# THE WAY TO UNITY

A Guide To Self Realization

Michaël Bijker

# Contents

| | |
|---|---|
| Introduction | 2 |
| Part 1 - What Am I? | 6 |
|     The different layers of our being | 11 |
| Part 2 - Cultivation of Awareness | 23 |
| Part 3 - Realizing Your True Self | 29 |
|     The Steps for Self Realization | 31 |
|     Levels of meditation | 42 |
| Part 4 - Practical Guidance | 44 |
|     1. Physical movement | 45 |
|     2. Pranayama breathing practice | 46 |
|     3. Meditation | 47 |
| Daily Living Advice | 49 |
| Afterword | 51 |

# Introduction

Life is a fascinating journey of experiences. For some, the experience is a joyful one, while for others it is one of struggle and confusion. How to make this life a blissful one is something that has intrigued me all my life.

I was driven to pursue a spiritual path from a young age for two main reasons: a desire to understand the nature of reality and truth, and to overcome health issues. Questions like "What is reality?", "What is eternity?", and "What is God?" always fascinated me, and I sought answers in philosophies and religions. This pursuit of spiritual understanding in religion and philosophy was both enlightening and satisfying, but it failed to fully quench my thirst for experiencing the truth firsthand.

Theories and explanations about life, God, and how we should live, however beautiful they may be, do not necessarily enable one to truly experience and embody the Truth. It is easy to say things like: "God is in everything and everyone", "All is One" or "love one another as you love yourself". However, when the mind is in chaos, the emotional system is blocked and the body is unhealthy, it will not be possible to experience it all, no matter how much beautiful theories or scientific facts you know. Knowing something with the mind does not mean you really experience and live it.

It is like someone who is on a journey and is eager to reach his destination. On his journey, he imagines what the destination will be like, he prays to get there and reads all sorts of things about it. Intellectually, he knows everything about his destination, while in the meantime, he has no clue where he is. His car is stuck in the mud and his vehicle is in a bad condition. He is not moving in any way towards his goal, and he is not even realizing it.

While it is important to know where you want to go, no matter how much you know about your destination in theory, it will not help you to get any further unless your vehicle is in good working condition and you know how to navigate your way.

For me this meant that, even if I knew all about life and reality in theory, my mind was still restless and I struggled with health problems that modern medicine could not treat. Not only did I need answers for the mind to fulfill an intellectual hunger, but also practices to heal my body and clear my mind. I felt the need for something more practical, something that would enable me to truly experience it all and improve my life.

I am grateful for the practice of Yoga, Meditation, and QiGong that came on my life path. It equipped me with the tools to clear my mind, make my body healthy and strong, and direct my awareness towards Truth.

This book is a collection of personal insights and interpretations from ancient spiritual texts. Parts of the book can be seen as a modern understanding of ancient Vedic texts and a practical and modern interpretation of the Patanjali Yoga sutras.

This book is written for those who want to improve mental and physical health, cultivate Awareness, and expand Consciousness. It is for those who want to realize the ultimate Truth and live a blissful life in connection with the Divine. It is for those who want to know their true Self and by knowing their true Self, know the essence of life.

With gratitude to Life, Creation and all the wondrous masters and souls that guide us in our lives.

May all be blessed with peace, love, and wisdom.

Michaēl Bijker

At the source of our being there is nothing to attain and nothing to fulfill. It is completeness itself that is both manifesting and experiencing life.

# PART 1
# What Am I

Everybody is looking, in one way or the other, for completeness, happiness and fulfillment in their lives, whether this is through material possessions, fame, acknowledgment or in spiritual practice. But where does the actual experience of fulfillment and happiness happen? It happens within this framework of the body, the nervous system and the mind. However, from a young age, we learn to find these qualities outside of ourselves, and many get lost in this search in life trying to find happiness in material things, status and pleasure.

Fulfillment, joy, peace, love and unity; all these states we look so hard for outside of ourselves are already present within us because these are the qualities of the source of our being. These are the qualities of our pure consciousness, which you are able to experience when you are able to let go of what is prohibiting you from experiencing your true self. When you can connect your awareness with that source.

## Freeing the awareness from the entanglement of the mind

So, how can we experience this, realize this and live life in line with this infinite source of joy and bliss? First let us take a look at why one cannot experience this profound peace, this state of bliss of pure being.

For most people, the mind and emotions are constantly fluctuating. When you close your eyes and try to become still, you become aware of how much noise and restlessness there is in the mind. There is a non-stop, chaotic firing of neurons in the brain producing thoughts, memories and imaginations.

The average person has about 60.000 thoughts per day, most of them are useless thought processes that consume one's awareness and take up mental space. The awareness is absorbed in these creations of the mind and is constantly bouncing from one thought to the other. In this way, there is no focus, no stability, no peace and one cannot bring the awareness deep into the moment, to the source of one's consciousness, preventing one from experiencing the bliss of pure Being.

## Merging your awareness with the source

When one is able to still the mind and focus the awareness on the present moment, on 'what is', on Being, one merges the awareness with the source of one's consciousness. This is union. The union of one's awareness with one's true Self.

In this realization, one experiences the completeness and bliss of 'pure being'. To realize this one has to bring the awareness beyond the veil of the mind. The awareness must be freed from the entanglements, limitations and creations of the mind. Through the mind, one cannot experience completeness. One can have theories, concepts and ideas about it, but the realization of it happens through awareness, through direct experience.

> Truth is not a story or an idea about reality, truth IS reality. Truth is not a philosophy, truth can only be directly experienced. It is what is here and now.

## Peeling off the layers that obscure the light of Being

Unity and bliss are the qualities of one's True Self, one's pure consciousness. A restless mind and emotional system prohibit one to experience this. One can try to experience the light of consciousness within, but all one experiences are the layers that cover up this light. Like a lamp that has gathered so much dust, mud and spiderwebs over the years, that one cannot see the light shining anymore. When one looks at the lamp, all one sees is those layers of dirt, but not the light of the lamp. One can try to make the lamp shine brighter by adding something to the lamp, but this does not work. The light is already there, but it is obscured. It is about clearing that what blocks the light from shining out.

It is similar to our internal lives. One can add things to one's life that one thinks will bring peace, love, abundance and bliss, but this is like trying to make that lamp shine brighter without addressing the root cause of the dimness. The light of Being, of pure consciousness is already shining within us. All that is needed, is to clear what prohibits one from experiencing this light within. One has to clear the impurities of the mind and emotional system, and to reconnect the Awareness with this light within and just BE in the purest form.

By stilling the fluctuations of the mind one will bring the awareness 'beyond the mind' and merge the awareness with one's True Self, with pure Being.

## The different layers of our being

You are a conscious, living entity of solid matter and energy, a mind, an emotional system and awareness. These are the five layers of our being.

### 1. **The gross body** (Annamaya Kosha)

We have a physical body. It is the vessel through which we experience life. This body is made out of matter (flesh, bones, blood, etc.). In a way, this is the soil of the earth that came together in the form that you are now, through the food you eat and the liquids you drink.

Your body is composed of particles that have undergone a journey through the cycles of nature, beginning as soil, plants, animals and ultimately originating from ancient stars. The energy that fuels your movement, thoughts and emotions comes from the food you eat, which is derived from plants that absorb the energy of the sun to create nutrients that your body can utilize.

You are the living soil and water of the earth that came together in a body that can move, think and feel with the energy of the sun. Your body is subject to constant change and transformation as a part of the larger interconnected universe.

## 2. The energy body (Pranamaya Kosha)

Without energy in the body, you would be a heap of lifeless matter. There would be no movement, sensations or growth possible. There would be no energy to move, think, feel, etc.

Different forms of energy are constantly flowing through our whole body. There is chemical energy to move muscles and fuel the body's organs. There is an entire network of electric energy that is flowing through the nervous system creating sensations, feelings and regulating bodily functions. In the brain, there are billions of neurons firing together producing thoughts, emotions and processing all sorts of life impressions. Every thought, feeling and emotion is a current of energy. This network of energy (prana) forms our energy body.

When this prana is not flowing in balance and harmony it causes disturbances in the body, mind and emotional system such as overthinking, anxiety, stress, and disease, among others.

---

You are not just a body of flesh and bones, you are also a body of energy. Those who can observe it, can control it.

## 3. The mind & emotional system (Manomaya Kosha)

This energy body produces another body; a layer of the self that is not physical and cannot be measured. However, we are all very aware of this layer of our being: the mind and emotional system.
The mind has several functions: to imagine (future), remember (past), calculate, distinguish, compare and judge.

Emotions serve as a way to enhance our experiences in the present moment, whether they arise from external circumstances or internal thoughts and imaginings. Additionally, emotions serve as an internal compass that helps us to distinguish between right and wrong.

Emotions motivate behavior, guide decision-making and determine our experience of this reality.

The mind and emotional system are intimately connected. Thoughts produce emotions and emotions trigger the mind to produce thoughts and memories and activate the imagination. This in turn produces more emotions. Thoughts and emotions are thus in a feedback loop. The body is intimately connected with the mind and emotional system. An emotional response reflects back on the physical body. A thought or emotion can relax or tense muscles in the body, change the breath, the heart rate and release certain stress hormones and neurotransmitters like adrenaline, endorphins and dopamine. A simple thought can cause the body to go into a state of deep relaxation or a state of stress. One can literally make oneself sick or healthy through their thoughts and emotions.

---

The mind is a powerful servant, but a terrible master. If one is not able to master the mind, one is bound to suffer the mind.

---

## 4. The 'higher self' (Vijnanamaya Kosha)

Every time you experience a sensation in the body, a thought or an emotion, who or what is experiencing this? When there is a thought happening (this talking inside your mind), there is also a part of you listening. When there is an emotion, there is also a part of you experiencing the emotion. This observer is your 'higher self'; it is the awareness that experiences mind, body and emotions.

When one becomes more conscious of how the awareness is constantly shifting with the fluctuations of mind and emotions, and cultivates the ability to still the mind and focus the awareness, one is able to transcend the awareness to the state of a 'higher self'. From this perspective, one can observe, influence and cultivate the mind and emotional system through wisdom, intellect and willpower. Meaning:

- one can choose where the awareness is focused on.
- one can choose the emotion produced by the emotional system.
- one can choose whether the mind is still or active.
- one can choose how the mind is behaving.

From the seat of the higher self one can regulate the state of body, mind and emotional system, and energy body.

When one's intellect and wisdom of the is developed well, one can choose one's destiny and not 'be lived' by the status quo of one's karmic states and life patterns.
To master this, one must first be able to observe all layers of the self and come to peace with 'what is' before attempting to control the other parts of the self. When one wants to control something they are not even connected with yet, it will only create more duality within.

You are experiencing thoughts,
but you are not your thoughts.
You are experiencing emotions,
but you are not your emotions.
You are experiencing a body,
but you are not your body.

You are both the experiencer and the experience of it all.

## 5. The True Self (Anandamaya Kosha)

> Consciousness is the divine source of creation experiencing itself.

This is the blissful source of our being. It is the source of consciousness that shines through all of us. Like light passing through tiny pin-needle holes in a sheet of paper that is held up to a bright light. These minute apertures may appear separate, yet they all emanate light from the same source and are part of the same sheet.

The paper itself represents the framework of matter and energy, or "the manifested", while the light represents the Universal Consciousness that infuses all of existence.
The combination of the manifested and consciousness form existence, which can be referred to as "Being", or Divine Creation. This is what we are in essence; both the manifested and the consciousness about it.

By directing our awareness back to the source of this consciousness, like looking through the pinholes back into the source of light, we can come to know our True Nature. This essence of our being is not defined by possessions, status, or ideas about oneself, but rather by the fundamental nature of Being itself. By realizing our True Self, we experience the inherent quality of profound bliss, inner peace, and fulfillment. We experience we are the divine manifestation of Creation/ God itself.

When one merges one's awareness with the essence in which everything is manifested and experienced, one realizes the Ultimate Truth.

I AM part of All and the All is part of me
All is One
All Is
Is
.

So there is:
- the Physical Body (flesh and bones)
- the Energy Body (energy that keeps the body alive, like the energy flowing through the nervous system and neurons firing in the brain)
- the Mind and Emotional System
- the 'Higher Self', through which one observes the other layers and make decisions using intellect, wisdom and willpower
- the True Self: Being/ Pure Consciousness/ Bliss body

## Cultivating the layers of the self

Every layer of our being is built up out of finer, subtler layers. The finer layer forms the foundation for the grosser layer and directly influences it. The cells, muscles, blood flow, etc. are directly influenced by our nervous and energy system. Our nervous and energy system is directly influenced by our mind. Our state of mind is influenced by a finer layer of subconscious mind, which, in turn, is the accumulation of past experiences and past mental and physical behaviors and actions (karma).

This can be influenced by our higher Self, which has the ability to use willpower, insight and wisdom to make changes within. At the source, there is pure consciousness and creative energy.

## A false sense of 'self' and the ego trap

There is another 'layer' of the self. I.e. the illusion created by the mind that one is one's possessions, the image about oneself and the image others have about him/her. This sense of self is an illusion, a construct of the mind. One can become so identified and attached to the possessions one has, that as soon as something happens with these possessions one suffers as if it happens to oneself. Or one gets so attached to the image other people have about oneself, that one will do everything to keep that positive image, even if it means living a lie, or giving up the quality of the other layers of the self.

One's entire life can evolve around this false identity of the self, and one forgets what one truly is.

## Bound to suffer

When one becomes fully identified with one's possessions, status and the illusions of the mind about their self-identity, suffering is bound to happen. Possessions will inevitably become outdated, lost or broken. People's perceptions and opinions will change, and the physical body will ultimately pass away.

Change is an inevitable part of reality in a universe that is constantly in motion. Without change, there would be no growth, no progress and no evolution. If one cannot let go and flow with the changes of life, then life will be one of struggle, frustration and suffering.

The remedy for this is to realize what one truly is, beyond one's material possessions, status and mental constructs. Through a deeper understanding of one's true nature and the impermanence of all things, one can detach from these attachments and attain freedom from suffering.

I look into the mirror
Silently I watch
And as the image is getting clearer
I let go
And set myself free
From all that I think I am supposed to be.

# Part 2
# Cultivation of Awareness

*We are like the nerve endings of an infinite body that experiences creation and itself.*

We are conscious and creative beings in an infinite field of creation. You are part of the whole, like the whole is part of you. Like a single cell in an infinite body that cannot understand or perceive the whole body, but can experience how it is part of it. We can sense our connection and the ways in which we are sustained by it.

## Awareness determines our life experience

Reality is an infinite field of existence, of Being. Awareness is the lens through which we experience a part of this infinite field of Being. This is what we call a 'life experience'.
The direction of one's awareness determines one's life experience. The awareness can be focused both outwardly and inwardly, i.e. on the world around us and on the five layers of the self.

When one's awareness is only focused on the mental constructs of the internal and external worlds, and not connected with the True Self, it can lead to feelings of disconnection, loneliness, depression, and anxiety. This can be compared to moving away from a warm campfire on a chilly night, and gradually losing the source of comfort it provides. While it may be tolerable at first, over time the cold can become all-encompassing, making it increasingly urgent to reconnect with the source of warmth.

When a person's awareness remains connected with their True Self and Being, they will feel connected, uplifted, energized and blissful.

## Deepening the awareness

One can train where the awareness is focused on. Focusing the awareness on one single object is called concentration. An untrained mind cannot concentrate and the awareness is bouncing from thoughts to objects, to emotions to thoughts, making it impossible to be fully present in the moment and merge the awareness with 'Being'.
Through training, one is able to deepen the awareness to the source of consciousness through the five layers of the self.

Like a light that gets focused to one single point into a laser beam that can penetrate through all the layers and veils that prohibit one from realizing the source of Being. When this is achieved, one unifies the awareness with the source of creation, Being, God, Great Spirit and realizes one's True Self.

## Bringing balance in the mind and energetic system

All thoughts, emotions and sensations in the body are streams of energy (prana) flowing through our energetic system. We can move and feel our hands because of the electrical signals flowing through our nervous system. Similarly, thoughts, emotions, imaginations and memories are all flows of energy that cause neurons to fire together. These flows of energy are like a river that is flowing. Sometimes this river is calm and peaceful, and other times this river is wild and turbulent.

For many people, this flow is imbalanced and disturbed causing unwanted sensations, restlessness, excessive thinking, imbalanced emotions and tensions. Like this, the experience of life is an unpleasant one. One is caught up in a struggle with how one <u>WANTS</u> to experience life and how life <u>IS</u> experienced. There will be a constant state of duality and internal conflict. One has to learn to both observe the flow of these energies and harmonize the energy system in order to bring peace in their life. Learn to observe the flow of this river and not be struggling with the river.

Come sit down and watch this river flow.
Sometimes high, sometimes low,
Sometimes fast, and sometimes slow.
Sit in the sun,
And leave your wings to dry.
You will have to dry your wet wings,
If you want to fly.

## What can cause an unbalanced state of being?

In order to bring harmony back into one's lives, one has to look at the cause of their unbalanced state of being and address it accordingly.

- Past impressions/karma. Every action one performs has a certain impact on the whole energetic system.
- False identification of the self as being the possessions one has and the idea one has about themselves.
- False identification of action and outcome. Thinking that certain behavior will give fulfillment when it actually does the opposite.
- Desire. When the mind is constantly saying fulfillment will happen at another time, at another place, under different circumstances. There can be no peace in the moment like that.
- Illness/imbalance in the physical and/or mental body.
- Habitual loops of thinking that are engraved in the energetic system causing one to think excessively and keep one's mind in a restless state.
- An imbalance in the emotional system causes some emotions to take over the entire field of awareness like: anxiety, guilt, shame, hate and grief.
- Unhealthy ways of living: too active or not active enough, laziness and wrong diet.
- Living out of alignment with the calling of one's heart.

# Part 3
# Realizing your True Self

## Steps to expand consciousness and be liberated from suffering

This is the method to purify (clear blockages and impurities) at all layers of the self, so there can be union and inner freedom and bliss can be attained. Oneness will be realized when there is the union of awareness, the observer, and the observed.

A journey to reach a destination starts with a desire and an intention. Let your intention be to cultivate inner peace and union with the source. One has to recognize that the state of life and being as it is, is not serving their full potential. This desire will be the fuel for willpower to keep doing these techniques even if it might sometimes be unpleasant or the mind starts resisting. It is especially in these moments where the mind resists that one has the opportunity to break free from old habits and patterns. It is like re-routing the energetic system from habitual flows that actually do not serve you, like addictions, counterproductive emotional patterns and patterns of thinking. One has to free oneself from this.

There must be both a desire for union within and union without, as well as a desire to become free from suffering.

One has to be willing to see the truth about oneself and the source of their suffering.
Also, one must seize all actions that add negativity to mind, body and spirit. When the bathroom is flooding, will you start by moping the floor or will you first turn off the tap? Like this, one should first stop the source of the problem by quitting any impure behavior.

Know your goal and discriminate between actions that facilitate reaching the goal and those that will hinder it.

# Steps for Self Realization

## 1. Adopting a lifestyle that fosters well-being, inner peace, wisdom and self-realization (Yamas & Niyamas)

Take good care of this body, the vessel through which life is experienced. The state of your body, mind and energy system will greatly determine the quality of your life. Take care of what you put into your body and what you put into your mind. Eat wholesome and nutritious food. Do not only eat to satisfy the senses, but nurture the body. Do not eat too much, nor too little. One should rest enough, but not be lazy, and have sufficient exercise for mind and body.

To see real progress, it is important to be consistent and determined in cultivating mind and body. Daily practice is essential for self-realization, and, as you progress, you will see a beautiful change in your life.

Generosity, kindness and doing good to others will give benefits to all levels of your life.

Cultivate gratitude for everything, both for what is perceived as positive and negative. Everything you can be thankful for will become a blessing for you.

Bring your awareness to that what is greater than yourself and contemplate nature, creation, the universe, and God. Doing so helps one to shift focus from minor problems and your 'small self' to your "Great Self".

Treat all life with respect. Don't do unto others what you don't want to be done unto you. Don't harm yourself, others, living beings or nature. Don't use or take more than you need.

Live in line with the truth. Lying, cheating, stealing, etc. will not bring the mind peace for it will create a barrier between yourself and the truth. Live truthfully so you have nothing to hide.

Every action has an effect on your energy system. When one develops more sensitivity to this by cultivating awareness, living more healthily and training the mind, one will feel the subtlest results of every action one performs. This will be the compass that will lead one to a blissful life. This will guide one to know whether an action is fruitful and in line with your intention (developing a life of bliss and inner peace) or counterproductive.

Everyone has this compass within, but for most, it is obscured by the noise of the mind, desire, fear and the inability to feel the subtle layer of one's being. When you eat something, learn to feel in the hours after what this does with your energetic system. When you say something, how does this make you feel? Whether you speak truthfully, negatively, or with kindness and love, it profoundly impacts your subtle bodies.

Establish a profound relationship with Life/ Creation/ God and see the interconnectivity of all things. Don't waste life energy on and use your life energy in line with what is right and what is good.

## 2. Physical exercises and postures (Asanas)

This body is the vessel with which you experience this life. If you have no energy, are ill, or have lots of tension, practicing meditation and living a blissful life are not possible.
Practices like Yoga asana, QiGong, Tai Chi or any kind of practice in which one mindfully strengthens and stretches the body is a must to bring the body in good condition to have enough energy and to have all the systems of the physical, mental and energetic body balanced and open.

Regular daily practice will also improve one's mental focus and clarity, fortify willpower and break free from habit patterns of laziness and loops of thinking and feeling. It helps one to take the awareness out of the mind and into the body and present moment.

There is an intimate connection between the physical body, the mind and the emotions. When there is tension in the mind, there will be tension in the body. For example, when one has a worrying thought, muscles in the eyebrows and lips contract. It might also tense up the muscles in the shoulders and other parts of the body. If the thought is very worrisome it will also release stress hormones like adrenaline and increase the heart rate, breath rate and blood pressure.

Stretching and strengthening one's physical body with kind awareness will also open up and strengthen the whole energy system. Physical exercise influences all layers of one's being, not only the physical, but also the mental and emotional layer.

The physical practices, breathing practices and meditation should be done in a place where one will not be distracted, protected from the wind, intense sunlight and insects. This will enable one to fully immerse oneself in the practice and the subtle sensations of the body without any distractions. Before starting your practice, set a clear intention to cultivate the mind and awareness, and commit to maintaining full awareness throughout the entire session.

## 3. Bringing the awareness within (Pratyahara)

One must develop the ability to bring awareness within, meaning to become aware of all sensations within the framework of one's own body and energy system. One should become aware of the subtlest sensations that constantly flow through all layers of our being, such as our skin, fingertips, muscles and every part of our physical body.

One then becomes aware of the state of the energy body. Is it restless or calm? Are there lots of thoughts and imaginations in the mind? Is the body peaceful and balanced, or agitated? Observe these flows of energy with kindness, compassion, patience and free from judgement. Let the awareness take the position of the higher self, and gently smile at whatever state the other layers of the self are in. Feeling is connecting. When one can truly feel and experience the layers of the self, one connects with them and can then influence them through various breathing techniques called pranayama (Prana= Life energy, Yama= to control, Ayama= to extend)

## 4. Inner cultivation through breathing (Pranayama)

Once the body is more open and strong and the awareness is established within, one can start using the breath to activate, unblock and harmonize the subtler layers of one's being.

These breathing practices involve both strong and subtle breathing techniques.

Strong breathing (hyperventilation) practices are great for the novice practitioner with a restless and untrained mind that requires stimuli to focus one's attention, and to come out of the thinking mind. These stronger practices are a powerful way to unblock, open up and activate the mind, energy and emotional system.

Many people are drawn to strong and intense breathing techniques because they produce powerful sensations and a euphoric feeling. It may also give a strong emotional release. However, it is important to
remember that these practices should not be overused and must be balanced with calm, gentle and slow breathing techniques.

The strong breathing techniques activate and unblock the energy system, whilst calm and slow breathing techniques will harmonize and balance it.

Strong breathing techniques will give a lot of mental stimuli and sensations, but, at the root level, the mind is not trained and the awareness not sharpened. When the mind is not stilled and the awareness not sharpened, the practitioner is still unable to experience the subtlest sensations which is essential for taking the awareness deeper within.

To balance the energy system, sharpen the awareness and still the mind, slow breathing techniques are essential.

Whilst doing hyperventilation breathing practice has its benefits, doing too much of it can have adverse effects, including the following:

- It can make the mind and energy system more restless in daily life.
- It can overstimulate the nervous system and bring disbalance in the emotional system.
- Because one is controlling the breath with force, one can increase duality within and pride, ego and self-centredness will grow.
- The awareness becomes dull, and one will not be able to feel the very subtle layers of being which is essential for deeper states of meditation.
- One can burn too much energy (prana) resulting in feeling low on energy in daily life.

## Using the breath to activate, purify and balance

The pranayama breathing techniques are like fanning a fire to achieve the ideal temperature. Similar to grilling food on a barbecue, there will be excessive smoke and insufficient heat to cook the food when the coals are not hot enough. If this happens, one must fan the fire to increase the temperature. However, if the fire is fanned too much, the temperature and flames will become too high, resulting in burning the food and quickly burning through the coals.

Similarly, one may also use powerful breathing techniques to release energy, ignite the fire within and burn impurities. However, it is important not to overdo it as it can lead to overstimulation of the energy system and mind, resulting in 'wild flames', i.e. overactivity and fluctuations in the mind. One can even burn too much prana (life energy) within, resulting in sickness, weakness and burnout.

Concluding, the breath should be used to both enhance and tame the fire within, and is to be done with care, kindness and patience. After strong breathing practices, slow breathing practices should always be followed. Additionally, it is important to set an affirmation of bringing peace, gratitude and unity within. All these practices help the mind to center the awareness, leading to the realization that all is a part of the same totality, and that totality is a part of us. The more advanced the practitioner becomes, the less forceful and more subtle the pranayama practice becomes.

One starts working more on a subtler level of one's being with gentle and slow breaths, with full awareness and pure intention. In this way, one balances and harmonizes all layers of one's being and sharpens the mind to enter into profound states of awareness.

These practices are called Pranayama. Prana means life energy. Yama to control. And Ayama to extend or lengthen. It is not only about controlling the breath. It is about expanding and lengthening one's breath to expand life energy and consciousness.

## 5. Centering the awareness, going deeper within and letting go (Dharana & Dhyana)

Now that the whole energy system (nervous system, mind and emotional system) is balanced, and the awareness focused and sharp, one can let go of any control of the body and breath and focus the awareness on 'what is here and now'.

If the mind is still fluctuating a lot, one should go back to the previous step of calm pranayama practice. Meditation is a quality that cannot be forced. It will happen when all systems are harmonized.
Attempting to force meditation is counterproductive for it is one part of the mind trying to force another part of the mind to behave in a certain way. This is a state of DUALITY that leads to inner conflict and frustration. What we want to create is UNITY and this happens through kindness and surrender.

With a kind and gentle effort, one can merge the awareness with the present moment, focusing on what is here and now, such as the sensations of the breath or the body. These sensations are the direct experience of reality, while thoughts, memories and other mental phenomena are mere creations of the mind. By continuously bringing our awareness out of the mind and into the present moment, one's awareness is freed from the confinements of the mind. The awareness becomes clear and concentrated, like a laser light that can penetrate through the layers of our being to reach the source of one's consciousness.

To truly experience the fundamental truth of our existence, one must learn to effortlessly concentrate and merge the awareness with here and now/ Being. Through this process, we come to realize that all is a manifestation of Life, a manifestation of God, and that in essence all is one.

Feel
With Pure Awareness
Feel
Through direct experience
And Feed
This consciousness
With the direct experience
Of what IS
Right HERE
Right NOW

## 8. Union (Samadhi)

When one has gone through the steps of; harmonizing one's energy system, stilling the mind, and merging the awareness with 'What Is'/ Being, one enters into a state of absorption in Being. By maintaining this state one merges one's awareness with the source of Being i.e. Pure Consciousness, Bliss, Ultimate Truth, Creation, God, the I AM.

All of this is now a direct experience. It is not "I" experiencing the "All". There is only the totality of Being, the unity of Pure Consciousness. This realization is the ultimate knowledge, the ultimate liberation, and the ultimate Self-realization.

---

I am part of totality, like totality is part of me. Therefore, when I truly know myself, I will know the totality as well.

---

# Levels of meditation

There are different levels on which the awareness can be merged.

1. A pleasant calm state in which one is able to keep the awareness in the present moment, observing the body and its sensations and the mind and its creations, directly experiencing life as it is, devoid of the filters and creations of the mind.

2. The mind is becoming completely still and one is able to observe all the sensations of the body in minute detail. One can feel the energy body in its pure form and purifies the karmic imprints it carries by shining the light of awareness onto it with equanimity. One merges the awareness with 'what is now', and experiences the peaceful infinite space of Being in which all is manifested.

3. One's awareness goes beyond the layers of self and experiences all is a manifestation of Being, the I AM/Divine Creation, in an infinite field of consciousness. There is no more identification with a construct of the mind about a 'self' that experiences. There is total unification of self with True Self/Being. The coming home of the spirit to its source. Only pure consciousness remains, pure bliss.

4. One goes beyond 'experience', because all experience is a construct. Beyond the construct of space and time. All Is and Is Not.

Existence, this what is, has no limits. No beginning and no end. It is both the source of manifestation and the manifested. The mind cannot comprehend this. The mind needs a reference point, a limit, to know what something is. Consciousness on the other hand experiences it. When one becomes pure consciousness, one becomes limitless.

# PART 4
# Practical guidance

## Set a daily life routine

To live balanced, connected and healthy one must implement daily routines and habits into their life. Taking time to care for your mind and body should be just as habitual as brushing your teeth, it should be done twice a day.

- When waking up, set your intention for that day: learn, be joyful and explore life as a gift. This will be the foundation of the rest of your day.
- Have a set routine for the morning! So when you wake up you do not have to THINK, you just DO.

<u>Daily Routine:</u>

1. Get up and wash your face/ body.
2. Drink a glass of lukewarm water with a squeeze of lemon juice. This helps to clean the body.
3. Take at least 5 minutes to open up and strengthen the body.
4. Do at least 10 minutes of Pranayama followed by meditation and connect with your source.

# 1. Five Tibetan rites

This ancient Tibetan yogic practice should be done daily and will increase one's flexibility, strength and overall well-being. The 5 exercises are to be done at least 9 times each. (One can practice to do this up to 21 times.)

### 1. Spinning clockwise 9 times with the arms out
Rotate 9 times. Then stand with hands together in front of the chest for 5 calm & deep breaths.

### 2. Leg lifts
9 leg lifts with slow & deep breaths. Then relax for 5 breaths in corpse pose.

### 3. Spine & heart opening
9 slow & deep breaths while opening up the spine. Then relax for 5 breaths on the knees.

### 4. Reversed tabletop pose
9 slow & deep breaths pushing the hips up. Then relax for 5 breaths.

### 5. Up & down dog pose
9 deep & slow breaths pushing buttocks up and down. Then relax for 5 breaths on the knees.

### Feel & connect
Bring your awareness within. Take some calm deep breaths. Feel and connect with your body and breath.

# 2 Pranayama practice

After opening up the body, sit comfortably with your spine straight. Connect the awareness with the breath, and the breath with the energy system.

## Strong Spinal Breathing

### Connect with the breath
Sit comfortably with the spine straight. Connect the awareness with the body and the breath.

IN  9 x  OUT    Hold OUT    Hold IN

- Breathe fully in for 3 seconds as you slide the hands to the hips and open the heart. Breathe out for 3 seconds, slide hands to the knees, round the spine. Repeat for 9 breaths.
- After your last inhalation, fully exhale. Contract the perineum, bring the chin down and lift the diaphragm (The Great Lock). Hold your breath OUT for as long as you comfortably can.
- Then take a full inhalation as you bring the head fully up, then bring the chin down again and apply The Great Lock and hold your breath IN for as long as you comfortably can.
- Take some breaths to observe and let everything settle.
- Repeat for 3 rounds

### Harmonize with the breath
Relax, let everything settle and calm down. Then breathe calmly, subtly and friendly for 5 minutes with a ratio of 2 : 1 : 2 (e.g. 6 seconds IN : 3 seconds HOLD : 6 seconds OUT). Make the breathing more and more subtle and breathe with full awareness.

# 3 Meditation practice

Now that the mind, nervous system and energy system are balanced through pranayama practice, it is prepared for meditation.

Sit with a relaxed, gentle and kind attitude. Focus the awareness on one single point, starting with the air coming through the nose cavity. Feel as the flowing air touches the inside of the nose. How does it ACTUALLY feel? Center the awareness there for some breaths.

Once the awareness is centered, move the awareness through the face. Take a moment to feel the eyebrows and allow them to relax, move the awareness to the muscles in your cheeks, lips, tongue, and jaw, observing any sensations you may feel. Continue to scan your body from head to toe without labeling or naming specific parts or sensations. Directly feel the sensations that are present in the here and now, without judgment or analysis. Become fully present of the sensation of being alive, here & now. Do not force your concentration or judge any feelings or sensations. Just feel "what is". Thinking some feelings should be there and others shouln't. What is judging what? Who is trying to control whom? It is one part of the mind trying to control another part of the mind.

If the mind wanders, just notice it and do not engage or fight with it. Smile at the creations of the mind and re-focus your awareness on what is here & now; the sensations of the body. Just like a cat that is sitting in front of a mouse hole, fully concentrated. He hears what is happening around him, his ears might move, but his awareness is pinpointed to the mouse hole. Like this let your awareness be fully focused on what is here & now.

When you have merged your awareness with the sensations in your body, experience the subtler and subtler sensations and layers of your being. Let go of any effort to focus. Let your awareness effortlessly flow and go deeper. Now BE for some time, just BE and realize the infinite space of Consciousness that is your essence.

End the meditation by generating contentment, love and gratitude. Take this awareness and relaxation with you into the rest of your day.

# Daily living advice

In order to make lasting changes in your life, it is important to cultivate daily practices that support your mental, physical and spiritual well-being. Establishing a routine will help you stay consistent and motivated in your efforts. Here are some advises that you can incorporate into your daily life:

- Have a daily routine of doing the movement, Pranayama and meditation practices at around the same time.

- Throughout the day, create habit patterns for the mind to be present, focused and in peace. To do so apply the STOP method: **S**top whatever you are doing – **T**ake some deep breaths – **O**bserve and connect with the moment (what are you actually doing and how are you feeling?) – **P**roceed mindfully

- Cultivate gratitude to God for everything. Apply this in all moments and situations in life.

- See every moment as an opportunity to grow. When something comes up that scares you, for example, use that moment to conquer your fears.

- Take some days, or at least some hours, of 'no-screen time'. So leave your phone at home sometimes, or just turn it off for some hours.

- Stop watching the news.

- Incorporate a moment of gentle breathing and meditation in the evening.

- Before falling asleep, when laying in bed, go through your day. What have you learned, what can you improve and what are you grateful for? Take a couple of nice deep breaths, generate a state of acceptance and gratitude and bring that state into every layer of your being.

By incorporating these daily practices into your routine, you will cultivate greater peace, happiness, and well-being in your life.

# Afterword

This book provides you with the necessary tools to develop your mind and body and awaken your life. However, it is up to you to take action and incorporate these techniques into your daily routine. Think of this book as a map that can guide you towards a more fulfilling life, but ultimately, it's you who must take the steps to reach your destination.

For more in-depth learning, visit www.yogalap.com. There, you'll find comprehensive information about our online courses and retreat programs that are designed to help you develop a more joyful and fulfilling life. Join the Life Awareness Project and awaken your full potential.

Printed by Amazon Italia Logistica S.r.l.
Torrazza Piemonte (TO), Italy